What Becomes

The Blackglama Story by Peter Rogers

a Legend Most?

Photographs by Richard Avedon and Bill King

Introduction by Erla Zwingle

SIMON AND SCHUSTER
NEW YORK

Photographs by Richard Avedon:

Lauren Bacall
Melina Mercouri
Bette Davis
Barbra Streisand
Judy Garland
Joan Crawford
Lena Horne
Marlene Dietrich
Leontyne Price
Rita Hayworth
Maria Callas
Barbara Stanwyck

Rosalind Russell
Claudette Colbert (pg. 43)
Paulette Goddard
Ruby Keeler

Photographs by Bill King:

Carol Channing
Pearl Bailey
Carol Burnett
Ethel Merman
Peggy Lee
Liza Minnelli
Diana Ross
Mary Martin

Beverly Sills
Raquel Welch
Graham, Nureyev, Fonteyn
Lillian Hellman
Shirley MacLaine
Suzy Knickerbocker
Liv Ullmann
Diana Vreeland
Faye Dunaway
Claudette Colbert (pg. 87)
Joan Fontaine
Helen Hayes
Renata Scotto
Angela Lansbury

Designed by Ken Sansone
Manufactured in the United States of America

1 2 3 4 5 6 7 8 9 10

Library of Congress Cataloging in Publication Data

Rogers, Peter, date.
What becomes a legend most?
1. Advertising—Mink fur industry—United States.
2. Advertising campaigns. I. Avedon, Richard.
II. King, Bill. III. Title.
HF6161.M54R64   659.1′13′0973   79-17194
ISBN 0-671-25077-9

The Introduction originally
appeared as an article in
American Photographer,
December, 1978.
Blackglama® is a registered trademark of the Great Lakes Mink Association.

This book is dedicated to Jane Trahey,
who conceived the "What Becomes a Legend Most" concept.
And to Henry Wolf, Norman Sunshine, Len Favara,
Richard Avedon and Bill King, whose combined efforts
have made Blackglama the Legend that it is.

ACKNOWLEDGMENTS

I would like to acknowledge and express my deep appreciation
to the following people for making this book possible:

Richard Avedon, photography (1968–1972)
Bill King, photography (1972–present)
Jane Trahey, campaign concept
Henry Wolf, art direction (1968–1971)
Len Favara, graphic design (1971–present)
Heni Abrams, for her invaluable assistance
in writing the Blackglama story

What makes one a legend as opposed to a star or a mere celebrity? The answer is complex—and hard to articulate. Basically, it's a matter of genuine, lasting achievement. Some legends are made virtually overnight, with a single act or performance. Others take years, even a lifetime, to develop. It doesn't always have to do with physical presence—a voice can be lengendary, a literary talent likewise. But all legends share a timelessness, a glamour, an endurance that goes beyond what's current or merely in vogue.

The thirty-eight legends who have appeared in the Blackglama campaign to date have all this in common and more. While I personally don't admire them all equally, there's no denying that as a group they comprise the most illustrious list of names ever brought together for commercial purposes. Names which, even more to the point, are seldom linked with commercial ventures at all.

Choosing legends is ultimately a purely personal and subjective pursuit. Obviously, there are many we've yet to capture—Hepburn, Taylor, Garbo, Onassis, Sinatra and Hitchcock, to name a few. Some have even turned us down flat. But as long as the people at Blackglama agree, and as long as there are legends, there will be a campaign. After all, what becomes Blackglama most?—a legend, of course.

The Raw Material of Luxury

For centuries fur has carried the cachet of luxury, and while nobody today needs to wear animal skins simply to keep warm, the glamour and expense of fur, especially mink, have ensured its position as a classic status symbol. Particular furs have always gone into and out of style (fox was the big seller in the thirties and forties), but by the late sixties the fur industry as a whole was facing hard times. Except for wearing the odd third-hand rabbit coat from the thrift shop, the counterculture shunned furs as ecologically and economically offensive. Environmentalists were hard critics of trapping methods, and the general public began to favor more casual styles.

Thus in 1968 the Great Lakes Mink Association (GLMA), a group of about four hundred ranchers who produce thirty thousand black mink pelts annually, searched for an advertising agency that would remodel public opinion. John Adkins, then advertising chairman of GLMA, chose New York advertiser Jane Trahey. Trahey conceived the campaign, which was implemented by her sharp young associate, Peter Rogers.

"Pete was just a young kid, a farm boy from Hattiesburg, Mississippi," recalled one executive, "but he was aggressive and had some good ideas." Rogers, who has since bought out Trahey and formed Peter Rogers Associates, put it simply: "The luster of the fur doesn't show up in a photograph, so Jane thought up a gimmick." The gimmick was to show the luster of the glamorous people who wear mink.

The major challenge was to create recognition for the fur itself. Blackglama (a name Trahey invented) is not a designer, but the producer of the pelts. The format was simple: a portrait with a few lines of copy. It was the ideal design for photographer Richard Avedon, who worked on the account for the first few years. The series debuted in 1968 with Melina Mercouri, Lauren Bacall, Bette Davis, Barbra Streisand and Lena Horne. Because the ladies lived up to the sobriquet "legend," no captions revealed their names. The effect was immediate and powerful—a mere two years later, Blackglama was considered the most prestigious black ranch mink in the world. Soon after the series began, stores like Bergdorf Goodman were selling garments that carried the Blackglama tag, and customers were asking for it by name. Very few other luxury items—with the possible exception of Keepsake Diamonds—enjoy this measure of recognition for their raw materials.

While Jane Trahey initiated the concept, Rogers has stuck with a good thing. Only two changes have been made over the past ten years: the typeface was altered, and photographer Bill King replaced Richard Avedon. King has pleased his clients, but this campaign is clearly one that depends as much on the person in front of the camera as on the one behind it. Finding the subjects, and then cosseting them with limousines and the personal attention of Rogers himself, plays as large a part in the project as any technique during the shooting.

The photo sessions are as uncomplicated as the layout of the ads. "A session can last as little as five minutes," King said, "and usually not longer than an hour." The photographs are usually retouched.

There are no elaborate costumes. A selection of coats is supplied that complements the sitter's personality. "Most of the ladies, especially the older ones, don't want to spend a long time," added King, "and they usually have already done their own hair and makeup." Many sitters have long experience in films or on the stage, and have already arrived at their ideal "look." Rogers tries to get makeup wizard Way Bandy whenever possible, "But he's almost as hard to book as the legends." Each lady is remunerated in mink. A few take the garment off the rack at the shooting (Bette Davis did), but most wait to have a coat custom-designed for them.

Nowadays the agency doesn't have to look for prospective models. It has become a sort of status symbol among the superstar set to be identified as a "legend," and Peter Rogers Associates has to fend off importunate agents whose clients haven't reached the level of recognition the ads require. The ads run from September through December in *Vogue, Harper's Bazaar, Town & Country, The New Yorker, The New York Times Magazine, L'Officiel, Women's Wear Daily, W* and, interestingly, *Architectural Digest* ("that magazine stays on the coffee table for months"). Each year Rogers prints ten thousand posters of the ads, which are supplied without cost to the general public and to furriers who use them for window display.

Peter Rogers has done his work well. Not only is Blackglama the most popular black ranch mink, but the fur industry as a whole is booming again. Stores are selling garments made of anything from bassarisk to zoril, but mink remains the dominant type—still the champion, its luster as bright as ever.

In order of appearance:

1968

Lauren Bacall   Melina Mercouri   Bette Davis   Barbra Streisand   Judy Garland

1969

Joan Crawford   Lena Horne   Marlene Dietrich

1970

Leontyne Price   Rita Hayworth   Maria Callas   Barbara Stanwyck   Rosalind Russell

1971

Claudette Colbert   Paulette Goddard   Ruby Keeler

1972

Carol Channing   Pearl Bailey   Carol Burnett   Ethel Merman

1973

Peggy Lee   Liza Minnelli   Diana Ross

1975

Mary Martin   Beverly Sills   Raquel Welch

1976

Graham, Nureyev, Fonteyn   Lillian Hellman

1977

Shirley MacLaine   Suzy Knickerbocker   Liv Ullmann   Diana Vreeland

1978

Faye Dunaway   Claudette Colbert   Joan Fontaine   Helen Hayes

1979

Renata Scotto   Angela Lansbury

My first encounter with a legend was unnerving but instructive. I arrived at the Dakota in a rented car with a driver and asked the lobby receptionist to ring. "Miss Bacall will be down shortly," I was told. I paced nervously. It's not every day you meet Lauren Bacall, and my experience with superstars was limited. Moments later, the elevator doors opened and out she stepped—completely made up for the shoot and looking gorgeous. As we approached the car I'd left waiting in the drive, I saw her look it over critically.

"Is this any way to treat a legend?" she asked, in that sexy Scotch-whisky voice tinged with humor. Oh, God! I thought. This isn't going to be easy. But Bacall had made her point with a charming combination of style, wit and toughness that was completely disarming. I got the message. From then on, it was long black limos for Blackglama legends!

Halfway through the park, on the way to the photographer's studio, Bacall turned to me. "About the coat," she began, referring to the Blackglama mink she was to receive in payment for her photograph in our campaign, "it's to come from Maximilian."

Maximilian was then, as now, one of the world's finest furriers, but our contract called for a different furrier. "That's not our agreement," I told her.

"Maximilian," she replied firmly, "or no picture. You can turn the car around." Needless to say, she got her Maximilian.

At the studio, she got a big greeting from her old friend Richard Avedon, the celebrated photographer we'd chosen to help us get our campaign off the ground. Bacall has been a model and knows exactly what works for the camera, so everything went beautifully. By then, Henry Wolf, the agency art director, had arrived on the set, so I returned to my office, leaving the car to take Bacall home.

It was a wonderful photograph as far as we were concerned. Bacall reflected perfectly the glamour and elegance we hoped to capture in our ads. However, later I heard she'd laughingly complained to friends that we'd taken all the character out of her face by retouching out the lines she'd worked so hard to acquire. Lines or no, the strength of Bacall's classy face launched our campaign and established Blackglama as one of the world's great status symbols.

WHAT BECOMES A LEGEND MOST?

An exquisite extra-dark
natural mink
bred only by
the Great Lakes Mink men.
BLACKGLAMA®

Melina Mercouri was the second Blackglama legend, and this time I arrived in a black limousine. The desk clerk at her hotel announced that Miss Mercouri would be down shortly. I could hardly wait. At the time, Mercouri was not only an international star but a political figure of no small repute. Her troubles with the Greek government were front-page news, and for me this only added to her mystique.

Ten minutes later, the elevator opened and out stepped Mercouri—hair in curlers with a hairnet tied over her head. No makeup. No jewels. No glamour. She looked like a Milwaukee housewife on her way to the beauty parlor for a comb-out. Completely disillusioned, I thought, If this is a legend, the campaign is over before it begins.

The drive to Avedon's studio appeared to be great fun for Mercouri and her entourage of Greek-speaking dressers, hairstylists and makeup people. They chattered and laughed all the way across town, ignoring me as if I weren't there—which really didn't matter since it was all Greek to me.

At the studio, Mercouri and company disappeared into the dressing room. Half an hour later, she emerged—transformed! And that's the way Avedon captured her—the glorious, glamorous Earth Mother, hair blowing in the wind.

Thanks to Bette Davis, the truant officer of my hometown, Hattiesburg, Mississippi, spent a good part of his working career, flashlight in hand, chasing me up and down the aisle of the Saenger Theatre. I guess there's never been a Davis movie I haven't seen. So the thought of finally meeting her was very special.

My lawyer also represents Miss Davis, and it was he who made all the arrangements for her to pose for the campaign. She arrived in New York from her Connecticut home the night before the photo session at Avedon's. I picked her up the next day at the Plaza Hotel to take her to the studio. In the car, she smoked nonstop, and from our conversation I realized that Richard Avedon had once photographed Miss Davis in a blue dress. Though she remembered the photo well, she had not seen the photographer for many years.

Avedon was late for the shooting because of an abscessed tooth. Miss Davis took a seat at the dressing table to await his arrival. Within five minutes a rather robust little man arrived at the door.

"Dick, Dick—it was in blue!" Kiss, kiss, puff, puff. I bent over and whispered to her, "Miss Davis, that is not Richard Avedon; it's Eddie Senz, the makeup man."

She looked me straight in the eye and said, "Gawd, I knew I'd guff it!"

Ten cigarettes later, we had captured the legend.

WHAT BECOMES A LEGEND MOST?

An exquisite extra-dark
natural mink
bred only by
the Great Lakes Mink men.
BLACKGLAMA®

We photographed Barbra Streisand early in her career, when the legend was only a singing legend. In just a year's time, I'd seen her grow from a filler act at the Bon Soir Club in Greenwich Village to a Broadway sensation with her showstopping number in *I Can Get It for You Wholesale.* After *Funny Girl,* there could be no doubt. The lady was an original.

The day of the shoot, I arrived at Streisand's Manhattan apartment and was ushered into her library/music room. I was informed Miss Streisand would be down shortly. In our previous conversations, Streisand had been very concerned about her wardrobe for the session. "No wardrobe," I'd told her. "You and Blackglama, that's all we want."

Eventually a woman appeared at the top of the stairs looking very much like a tall Orphan Annie. "I've just spent the last hour waiting in the wrong apartment," I thought to myself. But no—the voice was unmistakable.

I was somewhat surprised at how unassuming she appeared. I guess I expected anyone who'd achieved such fame in so short a time to be completely impossible. But Streisand was a pleasure. Though I was kept waiting (not to mention Avedon, a legend in his own right), it was well worthwhile. The shot was a winner. Because eleven years later, requests are still coming in for reprints of the Streisand ad, more than we've ever received for any other legend.

WHAT BECOMES A LEGEND MOST?

An exquisite extra-dark
natural mink
bred only by
the Great Lakes Mink men.
BLACKGLAMA®

I met Judy Garland by chance one night in a New York club. She was living in Boston at the time and agreed to do the campaign, saying she'd be in touch. She kept her word. There must have been twenty phone calls before the evening she actually arrived.

I telephoned every hotel in Manhattan trying to book her a suite and finally had to settle for the Penn Garden on Seventh Avenue—the only hotel that would accept the reservation. I couldn't believe it!

On the day she was to arrive, I received still another collect call from Judy. She had no money to get to the airport and could not come. I'd gone this far and wasn't about to give up now. So I hired a limousine and arranged to have it deliver her to the plane.

The plane landed on time, but Judy didn't appear. Finally a crew member told me she was still on board signing autographs. The hotels may not have loved her, but the public sure as hell did, as was proved over and over during the next two days and nights.

I went onto the plane to get her and was surprised to see her in that red sequined pant suit she'd performed in so often.

At the hotel, the desk clerk claimed there was no reservation for Miss Garland. Apparently the management had had second thoughts about having her there. I sent Judy and the friend she'd brought along to the bar. In a rare fit of temper, I demanded that the reservation be honored, that I'd take full responsibility for Miss Garland's bill. She got the room.

Tony Bennett was appearing that night at the Empire Room of the Waldorf, and Judy announced that we were going. When she made her entrance, the audience went wild. She'd sent a rose and a note backstage to Mr. Bennett, and when he appeared onstage, he asked "the fabulous Miss Judy Garland" to take a bow. She did, and then took the mike right out of his hands and performed his entire show while he sat on the floor in front of the bandstand. The audience had come to see Tony Bennett, but I don't think they left disappointed.

After the show, Judy insisted we visit Mr. Bennett in his suite. We were hesitant, but there was no stopping her. Mr. Bennett couldn't have been nicer and seemed to genuinely enjoy Judy's company. Blossom Dearie was there, playing the piano, and some other people I didn't recognize. We were supposed to be at Avedon's at eleven the next morning, so by three A.M. I tried to persuade Judy to leave. But she wasn't budging, and I left her the car and took a cab home, worrying that she'd never make it to the shooting.

At ten thirty I called her from the hotel lobby. She sounded extremely groggy but said to come up, she wasn't ready. I wasn't prepared for what I found. The room looked as though a hurricane had hit it— vodka bottles everywhere, the carpet completely soaked, feathers all over the place. "What in God's name happened here?" I demanded.

"Peter, Peter, it was the pillows." Gradually I pieced it together. She and her friend had obviously gotten into a pillow fight; the evidence was hard to miss. Dismayed, I told her to shower and dress and I'd take her to the studio. Moments later there was a great crash in the bathroom, and Judy emerged with her feet cut and bleeding. She'd knocked all her perfume bottles into the shower. Fortunately, the cuts were superficial.

Somehow we got her dressed and to the car. While the stylists worked on her, I sent her friend back to the hotel to pack up and check out.

By the time we'd finished with her makeup and hair, she looked terrific and told us she was happy to be there. The photo session went beautifully. She sang along with one of her albums for an hour, as though she were on stage. Ultimately, we chose a nonperforming shot. Somehow it seemed to capture the Garland image more poignantly.

After the shooting, things changed for the worse. Once Garland realized the assignment was all over, she turned on us and became downright hostile, as though we'd let her down. She seemed to feel we'd used her, and that we were no better than all the rest.

She left with the Revillon coat she'd worn in the picture. It wasn't even lined, and I tried to persuade her to leave it behind so we could finish it properly. But it was hopeless to argue; she was determined to take it. She said it was great being in New York and in fur again, and left in the limousine for the airport. I never met her again in person, but later saw a photograph of her with her last husband boarding a plane to London, wearing the Blackglama coat, still unlined.

WHAT BECOMES A LEGEND MOST?

At five P.M. sharp (I'd heard that when she said five she *meant* five), I rang the doorbell of Joan Crawford's East 69th Street apartment, expecting a maid to answer. With me were three Blackglama coats, one of which she would choose for the ad.

The door opened and there she stood—the queen of Hollywood—in a cotton muumuu and rubber thongs, not a stroke of makeup, her long hair in a ponytail held by a rubber band. "Hello, I'm Joan Crawford," she told me, as if there were any doubt. She shook my hand warmly. Through all the years I would know her, it was always the same. "Hello, I'm Joan Crawford," and the hand would go out. It didn't matter who it was, from a waiter to Nelson Rockefeller.

Joan Crawford was one star who understood the role of the director. Before the session, she called Avedon to find out how she should look. He told her to comb her hair up like Audrey Hepburn's in the Givenchy perfume ads of the day, and not to worry about wardrobe. The fur coat would cover all.

But Crawford was not the type to leave such things to chance. One never knew whom one might meet in the elevator. She arrived at the studio (at eleven A.M.) in a black bugle-beaded dress and her fabulous diamonds. Naturally, she met someone. Jean Shrimpton, at the peak of her modeling career, was there when Crawford made her entrance. "You're just as pretty as I knew you'd be," Crawford told her. "And you've got freckles, too." Then she sat on a stool for thirty minutes and gave Avedon all the best Crawford angles.

Two days later, her secretary called to invite me to a dinner party Miss Crawford was giving at '21' for the people at Pepsi-Cola. I attended, of course, and was seated on her right. It was the start of a friendship that endured over the next seven years.

Enough has been said of her demands. She demanded no more from others than she expected— and gave—of herself. She was a true professional in every sense of the word.

Very little has been written of Crawford's humor and her kindness. She never did anything halfway, and that included being your friend. I've heard all the stories, but they bear little resemblance to the Joan Crawford I remember. I knew her only as a loving, giving friend who liked to have a good laugh, frequently at her own expense.

Once while *Mildred Pierce* was showing on television, one of the owners of '21' called her from home during a commercial and jokingly ordered a hamburger, medium-well, hold the ketchup. Before the movie ended, his order was delivered—from '21': where else?

We often went out together, and Joan once called on a Saturday to ask me to go with her to a Neil Simon matinee. I was busy and had to decline. I called her on Monday to ask how she'd liked the show. "I loved it, darling," she replied. "I got three standing ovations." Crawford got standing ovations wherever she went, and she deserved them.

I'm not a game player, but one night Joan Crawford decided to teach me backgammon. It was like being in front of a firing squad. By the time I left that apartment, drenched with sweat, I was exhausted to the point of saying whatever came into my head. The next day I called her to thank her for the evening, saying I'd had a good time. "I know you did, darling," she told me. "You finally got to call me a bitch!" And then she screamed with laughter.

I've always considered Lena Horne the most stylish singer of our time. I bought my first Horne album at twelve and made it my ambition then to see her perform live. When I finally did, at the Empire Room of the Waldorf shortly after I moved to New York in 1959, she lived up to my every expectation. Lena Horne onstage is an electric personality. Little did I realize I'd one day witness a private performance in Richard Avedon's studio.

Ten years later, I arrived at her West Side apartment to escort her to a Blackglama photo session. To my surprise, she was already dressed in the most exquisite Blackglama coat I'd ever seen. I immediately thought of the coat she was to receive for appearing in the ad.

"Miss Horne," I joked, "you certainly don't need another fur with the one you're wearing."

She looked me straight in the eye and said, "A lady nevah gits enough mink from a gentleman!"

At the studio, Avedon was set up and ready to go. Photographing a singer singing is very different from photographing an actress. Actresses pose and know all their best angles. But singers just sing! Avedon had the album *Lena at the Waldorf,* and while he snapped, Horne sang to her own record. It was a memorable performance. From it, we bring you "Lena Live!"

After the first twenty-five Blackglama coats and capes I'd sent to Miss Dietrich's apartment were rejected, I decided to present the next three in person. Surely I could sell her on posing in one of them!

I arrived and rang the bell, and the door opened about an inch. "I'll show these to Madame," a heavily accented voice informed me. A woman yanked the coats from my hands and slammed the door in my face. I waited in the hallway, feeling as though Speedy Messenger Service had just told me I was through.

Moments later, all three coats were handed back along with their carrying box. I packed them up and returned them to Maximilian, feeling certain that this photo session was never meant to be.

Somehow Avedon convinced Dietrich that it wasn't the coat but the legend in it we hoped to capture. Amazingly, she agreed to pose.

Three cancellations later (sessions called on account of rain), she arrived at the studio in her *own* limo, already made up and ready to go.

"Dahlink, bwing me a miwwoh."

An enormous mirror was produced instantly. Standing, peering into it, she personally arranged every hair on that coat until the image was right.

"Now," she commanded. Avedon clicked.

"Bwing me a stool." It was done. Seated, Marlene rearranged her fur, crossed her legs and pulled the coat back to reveal those famous limbs.

Her agent gasped. I gasped. I think even Avedon was surprised. Later the agent told me she'd been offered $150,000 to pose for a hosiery ad just three days earlier and had refused.

When the session was over, I thanked her and told her how exciting the shooting had been for us, especially since we'd gotten the beautiful legs.

"Dahlink," Dietrich told me, "the legs aren't so beautiful. I just know what to do with them."

WHAT BECOMES A LEGEND MOST?

An exquisite extra-dark
natural mink
bred only by
the Great Lakes Mink men.
BLACKGLAMA®

I'd always wanted to meet Leontyne Price. She's one of the great opera singers of all time, and we're both from Mississippi. She grew up in Laurel, thirty miles north of my hometown, Hattiesburg. I'd read a wonderful story she'd told in *Time* magazine, about how she'd gone home for a visit after her debut at La Scala. She used to sing gospel in the church choir in Laurel every Sunday, and as she was walking down Main Street, the preacher waved from across the street and said, as though she'd never left town, "Hi, Leontyne. Still singing?" My God, she'd just conquered all of Europe.

A year before I actually met her, I saw her in a Rome night club called Pepestrella. It was four in the morning and she was outdancing everyone else in the place. That same evening, she was to make her debut in *Aida* at the Rome opera house. I was staggered by her; she's a magnificent-looking woman—and she sure can dance.

So when her P.R. lady, Elizabeth Winston, called to ask if I'd be interested in Leontyne for the campaign, we jumped at it. She'd just opened the new Metropolitan Opera House in *Antony and Cleopatra,* and her picture was on the cover of every magazine in the country. We knew it was time to go beyond the legends of Hollywood, and Leontyne was the ideal choice.

I picked her up at her Manhattan town house, completely made up and wearing an Afro wig that made her look even taller and more imposing that she already is.

We wanted to photograph her in a great sweeping cape taking a diva's bow, but the cape turned out to be no bigger than a stole, so we left it to Leontyne to supply the drama.

She sang Puccini for an hour while Avedon snapped her, spoofing herself all the while with hilarious asides. "This lady's not too bad," she'd whisper in mock surprise, and roar with laughter.

When I brought her the proofs of the ad, she told me, "My momma's gonna blow her mind when she sees this!"

Leontyne has a great sense of humor which I've come to know well. Now, every time we go anywhere together, she'll turn to me as we enter and say, "Honey, let's show them how we do it in the South." And if anyone can show them, it's Leontyne.

WHAT BECOMES A LEGEND MOST?

An exquisite extra-dark
natural mink
bred only by
the Great Lakes Mink men.
BLACKGLAMA®

Rita Hayworth is surely one of the great beauties of the screen. The original Sex Goddess, but a class act all the way. We had to have her for the campaign. Not knowing anyone who knew her, I finally tracked down her agent and arranged it all through him.

On the agreed-upon day, I arrived at the Plaza to escort her to the shooting. Her agent was in the lobby, and as we stood chatting, the elevators opened and a slightly chunky middle-aged woman with close-cropped hair approached us. I thought it was his wife. Not until he introduced us did I realize it was Rita Hayworth.

At the studio, she changed into the dress I'd had made for her—an exact copy of the strapless black satin she'd worn in *Gilda* when she sang "Put the Blame on Mame." She danced like crazy through the whole shooting and couldn't have been nicer or more cooperative. She's such a shy woman, it's hard to imagine her married to Orson Welles or Aly Khan. Not until the music began to play and the camera clicked did she lose her reticence and become the Rita Hayworth I remembered.

The ad ran on a Sunday in *The New York Times Magazine.* By noon Monday, we'd had almost two hundred calls. It was the first time anyone asked who the legend was. (A lot of people guessed Anne Baxter.)

From pictures I've seen recently, Hayworth today looks so fabulous that the shot we got just doesn't do her justice. She's the one legend I'd most like to rephotograph.

WHAT BECOMES A LEGEND MOST?

An exquisite extra-dark
natural mink
bred only by
the Great Lakes Mink men.
BLACKGLAMA®

M

aria Callas. In the history of the opera, no other diva has inspired such a devoted, almost fanatical following. Or carried off the role of the temperamental prima donna with such aplomb.

That Callas was a legend was never in question. But how to approach her? I decided to leave that to Avedon, who was in Europe covering the couture collections. Somehow he made contact. He asked; she accepted. What could have been easier?

The hard part came in getting a mink to Paris for the shooting. Customs was a problem, and ultimately the coat came from Europe. I didn't attend the session, so it was with considerable anxiety that we awaited the arrival of the contact sheets in New York.

I needn't have worried. The shot was a sensation. Callas was so thin and so gorgeous that we all noticed a striking resemblance to Anne Bancroft—and so did the public when the ad ran. We were swamped with calls.

It could be argued that by the time we photographed her, Callas was more infamous than famous. And certainly, the legendary voice was past its prime. But for me, Callas represented everything anyone ever dreamed an opera star could be. She had it all.

WHAT BECOMES A LEGEND MOST?

An exquisite extra-dark
natural mink
bred only by
the Great Lakes Mink men.
BLACKGLAMA®

Most legends seem to wear their images like a second skin, so I was a little apprehensive waiting for Barbara Stanwyck to arrive at Newark Airport in the pouring rain. She'd agreed to do the campaign at her friend Joan Crawford's urging. Crawford had called her and arranged everything. All I had to do was carry through.

The plane was late and I was smoking too much, half expecting the tough bitchy broad of a dozen films to descend on me. Instead, out steps a gracious, rather retiring, publicity-shy lady who I later learned is called Missy by her friends. As I ushered her to the waiting limo, she couldn't have been nicer. All the way to the Plaza, in rotten traffic and torrential rain, still charming. I was beginning to relax— though prematurely, as it happened. The suite I'd reserved looked as though it hadn't been renovated since the Depression. I gritted my teeth, waiting for the full star tantrum; but Stanwyck was a perfect lady, and calm to the end. We soon had her settled in another, more suitable suite.

At the studio next day, everything continued to go well. Avedon gave the standard star greeting; hair and makeup went smoothly. We'd planned to photograph her *Big Valley* style, in Western gear and mink, but at the last minute, I'd found an incredible Blackglama toga—very complicated, with buttons all the way down one sleeve. (If you wore it to the theater, you'd miss half the first act just getting it off!) Avedon started shooting with Stanwyck posing like a true Hollywood glamour girl. But it just wasn't working. She turned to say so and—snap! we had it, a tough, no-nonsense picture. Vintage Stanwyck.

Oddly enough, Avedon hated the shot, and for once we disagreed. "It'll kill the campaign," he protested. "And anyway, she'll never go for it."

Several days later, over lunch in the Plaza's Oak Room, I showed Miss Stanwyck two photographs. In my left hand, one of the many pretty but ordinary glamour shots. In my right, the one I wanted to run.

"You have a choice," I told her. "You can look like your average Hollywood star. Or you can look like Barbara Stanwyck."

Without a moment's hesitation, she reached to the right.

"Run it," she said. "I've never seen that word spoken on a page before."

WHAT BECOMES A LEGEND MOST?

An exquisite extra-dark
natural mink
bred only by
the Great Lakes Mink men.
BLACKGLAMA®

In my mind, Rosalind Russell always was and always will be Auntie Mame. It wasn't just the one role. It was a quality she projected in all her films. She played the madcap lady with a finesse that, in a funny sort of way, gave her more control than the dames who played it tough.

I contacted her through her producer husband, Freddie Brisson, who told me she loved the campaign and would gladly pose for it. At the time, she'd been taking medication for an arthritic condition and it had somewhat bloated her face, though not her trim figure.

Avedon arranged the shooting in Los Angeles. I was not able to attend, so Dick handled everything. Russell wore white satin Norell pajamas, and Avedon made a sort of blanket of the fur and had her kick it into the air. It was a perfect shot—the quintessential Mame.

I eventually did meet Rosalind Russell at one of the "legendary lady" evenings produced by John Springer. She was being honored at a party at the Rainbow Room in New York, to which I escorted Joan Crawford. Though Miss Russell was in ill health at the time, she never let on. The lady had great style.

WHAT BECOMES A LEGEND MOST?

An exquisite extra-dark
natural mink
bred only by
the Great Lakes Mink men.
BLACKGLAMA®

CLAUDETTE COLBERT

I met Claudette Colbert at Kennedy airport two days before my thirty-sixth birthday. She was flying in from her home in Barbados just to pose for the campaign. I waited at Customs and was stunned by my first glimpse of the famed Colbert bounce, sable-clad, coming my way. Though I hadn't seen all her films, I certainly remembered *Cleopatra* and her Oscar-winning performance in *It Happened One Night,* made in 1934, the year I was born. It was clear that only one of us had aged. And it wasn't Colbert!

From our first encounter, I was overwhelmed by her wit, charm and impeccable style—an impression that's only grown over the years I've known her. She may have gained her fame as a comedienne, but Colbert radiates sex appeal, and has the energy of a teen-ager. To me, she's the epitome of a lady.

The day of the shoot, Claudette arrived at Avedon's studio completely made up and ready to pose. She's always done her own hair and makeup, and this was no exception. Though I didn't know it then, the lady hates being photographed. Inexplicably, she thinks she has just one good side. In truth, she doesn't have a *bad* side.

Avedon and I directed her pose and she graciously complied, though she didn't really agree with our direction. I accompanied her to the hotel after the shooting and she invited me to visit her in Barbados. I thanked her and instantly dismissed the invitation as a passing pleasantry.

When the contacts arrived, I was forced to agree with her assessment of the pose. The photographs were good, but not quite the Colbert image. I sent proofs to Barbados anyway, hoping I was wrong. Miss Colbert called a few days later and, never mentioning the picture, invited me to visit Barbados the following week. Wild horses couldn't have kept me away. She was a superb hostess, and I had a marvelous time. The photo wasn't discussed until the night before I was to return to New York. By then we'd become friends, and Claudette confessed that she hated the pose and hoped I'd agree to a reshoot.

Avedon was willing, so Claudette returned to New York and we rephotographed the ad, this time capturing a Colbert image we were all happy with, including our star. The year was 1970, but the look was straight out of *It Happened One Night.*

Seven years later, we again photographed Colbert for the campaign—and as you'll later see, nothing had changed.

WHAT BECOMES A LEGEND MOST?

An exquisite extra-dark
natural mink
bred only by
the Great Lakes Mink men.
BLACKGLAMA®

PAULETTE GODDARD

If Paulette Goddard had never made another film, her performance in the 1946 movie, *Kitty* would have been enough for me. So I was delighted when Joan Crawford offered to introduce me, and thrilled when Miss Goddard agreed to pose for the campaign.

On the day of the shoot, I met her at her midtown apartment to escort her to the studio. My image of her from her films was that of the sexy lady, the cute, cunning kitten who could really turn on the charm. And she really can! She looked terrific, with the same svelte, youthful figure of her old movies. Avedon's studio was just around the corner, so we walked over and with a minimum of fuss, soon had her settled before his camera.

Since Goddard was heavily into yoga, she decided on a yoga-type pose—hands raised Buddha fashion above her head, legs crossed under her. Not our usual style, but it seemed to work, and we all felt comfortable with it, including our star.

In those days, we credited the furrier, in this case Revillon, for the coat that appeared in the ad. When I took the photo over for approval, the Revillon people had a fit. Though they loved the legend, they felt the pose didn't show their coat to its best advantage. So rather than chance losing Miss Goddard's exuberant spontaneity in a reshoot, we rephotographed the coat on Avedon's assistant, making sure we got enough detail to please the furrier. Then we stripped the two shots together—Paulette from the waist up, Sue Mosel from the waist down. And thanks to some excellent retouching, no one ever guessed—not even Miss Goddard.

WHAT BECOMES A LEGEND MOST?

An exquisite extra-dark
natural mink
bred only by
the Great Lakes Mink men.
BLACKGLAMA®

Long before I met her, Ruby Keeler had married Al Jolson, had tapped her way through one Busby Berkeley movie after another and after a long career had gone into semiretirement on the West Coast. At the time I photographed her, she was starring on Broadway in *No, No, Nanette,* the revival that returned her to the public's attention after some years away from the limelight. Yet despite all the publicity and the years as a celebrity, Keeler was as down-to-earth and unpretentious as the housewife next door. In fact, it was almost impossible to think of this sweet, middle-aged lady as a tap-dancing legend.

We did her makeup at the studio, and she changed into the two-piece mink outfit we'd found at Bergdorf's. I had asked her to bring her tap shoes, and when she put them on—transformation! Those shoes started tap-tap-tapping and never stopped. They tapped like mad onto the set, through a full hour's photo session and back to the dressing room. I could hardly believe my eyes. It was like the story of the girl with the red shoes, the children's classic in which a pair of red dancing shoes possess their wearer.

Not until she slipped those shoes off did Ruby Keeler disappear once more and the nice little suburban matron return in her place. It was the damnedest thing I'd ever seen.

WHAT BECOMES A LEGEND MOST?
An exquisite extra-dark
natural mink
bred only by
the Great Lakes Mink men.
BLACKGLAMA®

Some performers become so associated with one or two major roles that it's hard to think of them in any other context. And certainly that's true of Carol Channing, at least for me.

Bill King and I traveled together to Washington, D.C., where Channing was starring in *Lorelei,* a latter-day version of *Gentlemen Prefer Blondes,* the show that catapulted her to fame. Her manager/husband had contacted us about using her in the campaign. (By now the legends were calling us.) We of course agreed at once. There's no denying Carol Channing is a legend.

On the appointed day, Channing arrived at the studio Bill had rented with her makeup man and hairdresser from the show. I was full of anticipation, expecting a combination of Dolly Levi and Lorelei Lee —bouncy, exuberant, outrageous and fun. And that's just what we got. We draped her in mink and masses of diamonds, and she sang her way through the session to "Diamonds Are a Girl's Best Friend." She worked damn hard, and the photograph was a great success. We'd tried for a leg shot (she's got wonderful legs and doesn't mind showing them), but ultimately it wasn't the best picture.

Some months later I was at home watching Johnny Carson, and Channing came on in the full-length white EMBA mink she'd received for appearing in the campaign. Nearly every other legend has chosen Blackglama, but Channing, she explained, wore only white. Anyway, as I sat watching in shock, she informed America on network TV that she'd appeared as a legend in the Blackglama campaign and here—indicating the white mink—was the coat she'd gotten for doing it. Knowing how hard mink breeders work and how early they rise, I realized the situation could have been worse. At least it was the *Tonight* show and not *Today.*

Years later, I appeared on the *Dinah Shore Show* to talk about the campaign. With me at Régine's, where the show was being taped, were a carload of Blackglamas and five gorgeous models. Carol Channing was scheduled to make a surprise appearance as a legend. To my despair, she arrived in white mink. "For God's sake, Miss Channing," I told her, "if you wear that coat on this show, I'll lose my client."

To my relief, she agreed to change into one of the Blackglama capes I'd brought along, and moments later she came on camera to huge applause. Otherwise, she might have brought an untimely end to a very successful ad campaign.

What becomes a Legend most?

Blackglama

Some people claim her big success in *Hello, Dolly!* boosted Pearl Bailey to legend status. But for me, it goes way back. Pearlie Mae is a true original and nobody else even comes close.

Since Crawford and Bailey were great friends, Joan asked her to do the campaign for me. She accepted instantly, with the proviso that she meet me first to get acquainted. She was on the road in *Dolly* at the time and flew into New York for just a few days. We met for lunch at Sardi's—her choice—and for the next two hours, Pearlie Mae talked and I listened. She talked about God, about show business and about *Dolly*. But mostly, she talked about Pearlie Mae. I must have been a good audience, because when we got up to go, she grabbed me, kissed me and said, "I knew I'd love you!"

How would she know? I wondered. I never had a chance to open my mouth.

The day of the shoot, she arrived with an entourage. We did her makeup there and she wore a black velvet cap. It made her look a bit like a cab driver, but she loves hats, so I agreed to it. I'd chosen a glamorous Blackglama cape for the ad, and it suited her perfectly. She looked marvelous.

She sang and talked nonstop for more than an hour while Bill King photographed her. She ran through her entire nightclub routine, and though we had the shot after fifteen minutes, it isn't easy to turn Pearl Bailey off once she gets started. By the time she left, with kisses all around, we were positively limp. She's got so much energy, it's exhausting to be with her.

There's a song Bailey sings that I've always loved. It sold me on her for the campaign probably more than anything else. "Tired," she drawls, "I'm just too tired. I'm too tired to put on my mink."

Whoever wrote those lyrics obviously never met Pearlie Mae.

What becomes a Legend most?

Blackglama

I

f you've never stayed at the Beverly Hills Hotel, you don't know what you've missed. People talk about the Polo Lounge, but it's the pool that's not to be believed. It's cabana-lined and very forties, where the famous and would-be-famous sit and have themselves paged over and over again all day. This was my first time in L.A., so you can imagine my surprise at hearing my name boom out across the pool. Sheepishly, I crossed to a phone.

"Hi, Peter. It's Carol." Anyone who owns a television set would know that voice instantly. We talked about the shoot and she asked if the photograph could show her legs, since she considered them her best feature. "They're all I've got going for me," she joked.

Mind! I thought it would be great. I offered to pick her up, but she declined, saying she'd meet me and Bill King, the photographer, at the studio.

On the day of the shoot, Carol arrived in a pickup truck with her hairdresser at her side and her Danskins in a brown paper sack. I had three hip-length Blackglama jackets with me. When I opened the box and pulled out the first, she shrieked in mock despair, "I hope I shaved high enough!"

The rest was incredible. As Bill King snapped, Carol took off on nearly every legend we'd ever run in the campaign and some we hadn't. Her Crawford *Torch Song* impression was the high point.

Carol Burnett is everything you hope her to be. She's that lovable, outrageous, funny woman you see on television. And a genuinely nice person in every way. There's no question that she enjoyed doing the campaign, but she's the only legend who ever declined the coat. Instead, she requested a donation be made to a charity in her name.

What becomes a Legend most?

Blackglama

If anyone deserves the title "Ms. Show Biz," it's Ethel Merman. Yet, ironically, no one could be more genuine and unpretentious than Ethel. She's an outspoken, steak-and-potatoes lady, who doesn't have a phony bone in her whole talented body.

I contacted her through friends who knew her, and she said she would be thrilled to do the campaign. I was certainly thrilled to have her. She's American musical comedy's leading natural resource —there's just no one like her.

The day of the shooting, things got off to a bad start, but Ethel was unflappable. Maximilian had mistakenly sent the wrong-size coat, and it didn't fit. So I redesigned it on the spot—pulled in the sleeves, draped it around her and pinned it in the back. Instant toga, and very effective. Ethel's got terrific legs, and we decided to show them.

While Bill King snapped, Ethel belted, "There's no business like show business. . . ." You could have heard her in Cincinnati. She even rehearses at full throttle. It's the only way she knows. She held nothing back, and it showed in the photograph.

The picture was great, and Ethel agreed. We became good friends, and later, when Ethel and Mary Martin starred together in a two-woman show, I sent her flowers and a note that read, "Now I know what legends are really made of." She called and told me she'd cried when she read it. It's a side of Ethel Merman that the public rarely sees.

What becomes a Legend most?

Blackglama

BLACKGLAMA® IS THE WORLD'S FINEST NATURAL DARK RANCH MINK BRED ONLY IN AMERICA BY THE GREAT LAKES MINK MEN

Peggy Lee was the only legend ever to send *her* car for *me!* An enormous gray Mercedes met me at my hotel and whisked me to her home, where she was being coiffed and made up for the photo session.

I waited in her living room, sipping tea, astounded by the number of people in the house. There were so many male assistants running back and forth, it looked like the locker room of the L.A. Rams.

Someone said Miss Lee wanted to speak to me. Before I could put down my teacup to go back to her dressing room, her voice came over an invisible intercom in stereo. "I won't be long," she told me. We proceeded to have a nice chat, though I still hadn't laid eyes on her.

In the last pictures I'd seen, Lee was quite overweight. So to be on the safe side, I'd brought along a huge Blackglama coat for the ad. Thirty minutes later, when she finally appeared, my mouth dropped open. She looked absolutely sensational—blond, petite and all of a size nine!

"Surprised, huh?" she laughed, and swept me along with her to the car.

We piled in—makeup man, hairdresser et al.—and headed for the studio to meet Bill King. Lee was wonderful in the car—funny, charming and terribly sweet. She talks just the way she sings, with that sexy, breathless quality that keeps you leaning forward to catch every word.

In front of the camera, she was a pro. She sang to her own records for nearly an hour, and we loved every minute. She's always been one of my favorite singers, the essence of a nightclub entertainer. So this private performance was a real bonus for me.

The photograph was glorious in the end. Miss Lee liked it so much that she used it, without permission, for publicity purposes for more than a year. I finally had to ask her to stop after I saw a huge blowup of it in the window of a discount record store—not the ideal setting for America's finest natural dark ranch mink.

What becomes a Legend most?

Blackglama

I find it almost eerie that so much talent should wind up in one family. But seeing Liza Minnelli in action made me a believer. Her Academy Award–winning portrayal of Sally Bowles in *Cabaret* ranks as one of the all-time great musical movie performances, and certainly one of my most memorable film experiences.

We were all excited about photographing Liza for the campaign. She was young and she was current, with a stage presence and a following that rivaled no one's if not Judy Garland's. I contacted her through her agent, and after some rather intense negotiating Liza agreed to do the ad.

The day of the shoot she rolled up in a battered old convertible with an entourage of friends, all having a grand time. I was surprised at her appearance. I guess I expected Sally Bowles instead of a real live girl. But an hour later, after hair and makeup, she emerged looking as glamorous and electric as she appears on stage and screen.

She seemed nervous about being photographed, but calmed down at once when Bill King turned on her records. For the next hour and a half, he snapped her as she sang. Watching her perform in that setting gave me the strangest feeling of déjà vu. It could have been Judy up there—the same mannerisms, the same vulnerability. The resemblance has never seemed so obvious to me before or since. I was ready to attribute it to imagination, but the contacts confirmed it for me. Out of rolls and rolls of film, there was really only one usable choice—the shot that focused on those enormous *Cabaret* eyes. Everything else was a dead ringer for her mother.

Liza Minnelli was one of the youngest legends we ever photographed, and certainly one of the most popular. We still receive frequent requests for reprints of the ad, along with a few letters complaining about the cigarette in her hand.

What becomes a Legend most?

Blackglama

I rang Miss Ross's suite at the Pierre, and a secretary told me she'd be down directly. She was—in an Afro wig the size of a serving platter. My reaction must have shown in my face, because she laughed and told me not to worry, she'd brought along a lot of wigs and would gladly wear whatever I selected. Not that she looked bad, mind you. I don't even think that's possible. It's just that it was a new Ross look for me. The lady has many looks, and all sensational.

On the way to the studio, she asked if I'd ever considered her good friend Cher for the campaign. (At the time, Ross and her husband and Cher and hers were traveling together, all staying at the Pierre.) I answered truthfully that I never had and probably never would, though her agent had called many times. "That's funny," she said. "I thought she'd turned it down."

When we arrived at Bill King's studio, Diana showed us everything she'd brought and said, "Okay, I'm in your hands. Just tell me what to do." We did, and she did it. The shoot was one of the best ever—and certainly one of the most fun. Ross sang and danced for about an hour, and Bill got an action shot so vibrant, it practically pops off the page.

Afterward, we went directly to Maximilian to pick out her coat. She tried on every one in the place and finally settled on a floor-length sable so chic it came complete with its own poplin rain overcoat. She said she loved all the Blackglamas, but already owned one, and just had to have this sable. It was a fabulous coat, but way beyond my client's budget, and my discomfort must have been obvious.

"Don't look so worried," she laughed. "I know it's not our agreement, but I'll make up the difference myself if it's all right with you."

Of course she got her sable. By that time, I was so in love I'd have agreed to anything, if only she'd thought to ask.

What becomes a Legend most?

Blackglama

BLACKGLAMA® IS THE WORLD'S FINEST NATURAL DARK RANCH MINK BRED ONLY IN AMERICA BY THE GREAT LAKES MINK MEN

Mary Martin believes—and rightly—that "My Heart Belongs to Daddy" is the song that made her a legend. But it was her portrayal of Peter Pan that's best known and loved by admirers of all ages the world over. We'd discussed this at length in several phone conversations prior to the photo session. Miss Martin wanted to re-create "Daddy" for the ad—granny glasses, hat, trunk and all. I tried to persuade her to be Peter Pan, but she was determined. So, of course, I agreed.

The day of the shoot, she arrived at King's studio with the glasses and a little fur hat she'd actually made herself. She's an adorable lady—trim, youthful and Texas all the way. She wears very little makeup, and we kept it that way for the camera.

Bill King photographed her sitting on the legendary trunk, and for an hour, she performed "My Heart Belongs to Daddy." "Now let's do it your way," she told me. I'd brought a little fur weskit, just in case, and produced it on the spot. Moments later, it was Peter Pan, not Mary Martin, in front of that camera. She really made you believe it.

When the contact sheets arrived, they confirmed what I'd suspected all along. The "Daddy" shots were cute, but the granny glasses made her look ninety, instead of the youthful way she appears in real life. I decided to send both shots to her California home to let her see for herself.

Two days later, she was on the phone. "You were absolutely right," she agreed. "Run the Peter Pan shot."

The ad received considerable attention when it appeared in the national publications. But the best reviews of all came from Miss Martin's own grandson. "Wow, Granny," he told her, "I didn't know you had such great legs!"

What becomes a Legend most?

Blackglama

At the time we photographed her, Beverly Sills had already sung at the Met and was probably the best-known, most acclaimed opera star in America. I'd heard her perform many times and had always come away impressed, above all, with her remarkable acting ability. If she hadn't been a singer there's no doubt she would have made it on the dramatic stage.

She was on tour and flew into New York just to do the campaign. I met her downstairs at Bill King's studio. After years of experience with legends, I expected someone small; they all look like giants on the stage or the screen and in person often turn out to be tiny. But Sills surprised me. She's a big lady with a big smile, and one of the nicest people you'd ever want to meet—easygoing, affable. Nothing of the prima donna in Beverly Sills.

We touched up her hair and makeup and settled her on the set. I was looking for fire and ice, the dramatic qualities I'd seen so often on the stage. But instead we kept getting Bubbles Silverman, the nice Jewish girl from Brooklyn, in what might have been her first mink coat. We just weren't getting what we wanted. Finally I stood behind her and pinched her. The hand flew into the air in surprise, and click! Bill King had the shot. It was exactly the look I'd planned on, and Miss Sills loved it too. I hope by now she's forgiven me that unchivalrous pinch.

What becomes a Legend most?

Blackglama

BLACKGLAMA® IS THE WORLD'S FINEST NATURAL DARK RANCH MINK BRED ONLY IN AMERICA BY THE GREAT LAKES MINK MEN

Raquel Welch was chosen to do the campaign for one reason only. Monroe she's not, but she's the closest thing we've had to a sex symbol since.

She'd arranged to meet us at Bill King's studio on the day of the shoot. I'd arrived early, as had Pablo, the legendary makeup man from Elizabeth Arden, and a group of us were sitting in the reception room having lunch and talking.

After a time, a woman in jeans and platform shoes, hair wrapped in a bandanna, no makeup, entered the room and wandered around for a while as we continued to eat and talk. Finally, with a start, I realized it was Welch. Our legend had arrived and we hadn't even recognized her!

As is the case with many stars whose on-screen persona is ten feet tall, Welch is actually quite tiny. She was friendly and pleasant through all the preliminaries, and by the time hair and makeup were completed, she looked fantastic. There was no mistaking her then!

She asked us how we'd like her to pose, and we told her the sexier the better. It obviously wasn't the right answer. Her hands flew to her face, and she indignantly replied, "This *face* is what made Raquel Welch a legend."

Once we had her settled before the camera, her attitude seemed to change. She worked really hard, tried everything we asked. And the results were sensational, as you can see. It wasn't exactly a head shot, but then, we never intended it to be.

What becomes a Legend most?

Blackglama

Graham, Nureyev, Fonteyn. Any one would have been wonderful. All three was a coup! I'd tried in the past to interest Nureyev and Fonteyn; they'd turned me down flat. So I was amazed when Miss Graham's agent called to offer not just his client but all three of the world's most famous dancers. Nureyev and Dame Margot were to dance in a Martha Graham benefit festival in New York, and in deference to Miss Graham had agreed to pose.

Bill King and I were so nervous at the prospect of a triple-legend shooting that he actually hired three young dancers to help us rehearse the shot in advance.

The day of the photograph, Miss Graham arrived by limo at the studio, already made up and ready to go. Dame Margot arrived in a second car and her makeup was done there. She's a delightful woman—exceedingly polite, beautifully dressed—with a regal air that's quite beyond the mien of ordinary people. And a quiet serenity that's a pleasure to be near.

Nureyev came straight from a rehearsal. I quickly introduced myself and offered him the lunch I'd had sent up from a caterer.

"I don't eat your food," he informed me bluntly. "I don't know you." Luckily, before long Monique

Van Vooren and a whole group of Nureyev's pals arrived with food from the Russian Tea Room, so our star didn't go hungry.

Eventually the three began looking through the group of more than seventy-five coats and capes we'd arranged to have on hand. Nureyev tried on every coat on the rack and finally chose one, an elaborate affair emblazoned with jewels and gold embroidery—the coat I'd preselected for Miss Graham. It was perfect for her, chosen to give the high-collared look she's so famous for. It wasn't until I'd produced the furry Daniel Boone–type hat I'd had made up for him—he loved it on the spot—that Nureyev relinquished the jeweled number to Graham and settled on another.

Fonteyn and Nureyev were skittish and a bit impatient before the camera, and we weren't getting anywhere. Finally, Graham commanded, "Rudi, Margot! You must behave. I need a new fur coat!" From then on, things went smoothly.

The three dancers posed, and Bill King snapped. After twenty minutes or so, Nureyev decided he'd had it. "Enough, finished," he exclaimed, and stalked off the set with Dame Margot hot on his heels. The amiable Miss Graham remained, however, and we shot a few more rolls of her alone.

It isn't easy to direct a group as strong-willed as the one we had that day. So ultimately we left it up to them to find the right pose. And it worked. Because out of all the chaos, the picture we got was far stronger than the one we'd planned.

What becomes a Legend most?

A Note from Peter Rogers:

For unknown reasons, Mr. Nureyev refused permission to reproduce the photograph,

Blackglama

Lillian Hellman is a legend in anyone's book. I'd always admired her and certainly wanted her for the campaign. But how to approach her? And would she be receptive? I had no idea!

Then I remembered that Hellman was to have lunch with Claudette Colbert that very day. I knew I'd never have a better opportunity and decided to give it a try.

I called Claudette and asked if she thought Miss Hellman might be interested. "I don't know, darling," she replied. "Send over the proofs of the campaign, including the one of me, and I'll ask her."

At exactly five past one, Claudette called and said, "There's a legend here who would like to speak to you." A deep, husky voice got on the line and said, "I know your town, Hattiesburg."

"I know your town, New Orleans," I replied, "and I'd like to know you. Will you do the ad?"

"My hair's a mess," she told me.

"Don't worry. We'll have someone there to do hair and take care of everything. We want you."

"All right. When?"

"How about now?"

"How about right after lunch?" And that was it.

I doubt Hellman would even have considered doing the campaign if it had not been that spontaneous.

Excited at this stroke of luck, I turned to tell my art director, Len Favara, who had just walked in. "You'll never believe it!", I exclaimed. "Lillian Hellman just agreed to pose for the campaign."

"Wonderful," he answered, looking a little vague. Moments later he turned and asked, "This Lillian Hellman—is she with the mayonnaise company?"

I picked her up at her apartment and liked her immediately. She's funny, direct and very much to the point. In the car, she smoked one cigarette after another, and at Bill King's studio she stuck the pack in the pocket of the fur coat and smoked all the way through the shooting. She seemed amused and obviously enjoyed the session.

A week later I took her to Maximilian to select her coat, and then to my office to see the pictures we'd shot. Happily, she liked the one I'd chosen.

Since Hellman is a writer, not a performer, we knew that almost everyone knew the name, but not necessarily the face.

However, the response was overwhelming. We got letters from all over the country. Some people wrote just to tell us how sexy they think she is.

As for the campaign itself, it was a real shot in the arm. The Hellman picture got editorial coverage in nearly every magazine in the country and brought international attention to the campaign, as well as over a million dollars of free publicity for my client. And that's not mayonnaise.

What becomes a Legend most?

Blackglama

Bill King and I decided in advance to try for a dance shot with Shirley MacLaine, and she agreed. She arrived at the studio with her dance clothes, looking adorable, exactly as I had pictured her. I introduced myself, and she was very bubbly and friendly. But it was downhill from there.

"I have a marvelous idea for the picture," she announced, pulling a pair of white majorette boots from her bag. They were just awful.

"No way," I told her. "Not in my Blackglama ad!" MacLaine has the most beautiful legs you've ever seen, and I knew those white boots against dark tights would have been a disaster.

"They'll make your legs look stumpy," I explained. Ms. MacLaine, however, disagreed, and a noticeable chill came over the proceedings.

On the set, MacLaine wanted a mirror set up behind the photographer so she could watch herself —an understandable request from a dancer. But Bill can't work that way and refused. In addition, he hates spectators on the set and asked her P.R. lady to leave. By now, the situation had become frosty.

MacLaine worked hard for the camera, nonetheless. We took a load of dance shots; head shots, the works—some in the black Charles Jourdan pumps I'd brought, and some (to keep the peace) in her white majorette boots.

When the contact sheets arrived, it was hard to make a choice. MacLaine is such a vibrant, vivacious personality that her best qualities are difficult to capture in a still photograph. In fact, most of the shots just didn't look like Shirley MacLaine. When it came right down to it, there was really only one that said it all.

I decided to show the picture I'd chosen to MacLaine for her approval. It wasn't specified in our contract, but I wanted her to be happy with it. She liked it a lot and graciously conceded the point about the shoes.

I've never regretted my insistence that day, because the MacLaine shot ultimately became one of the most popular of the entire campaign.

What becomes a Legend most?

Blackglama

Aileen Mehle is a paradox. Her entire livelihood depends on gossip, yet she's one of the most trusted people in her profession. You can tell her anything off the record and that's exactly where it stays. Small wonder she's been confidante to some of the world's most celebrated people. Not only is she gorgeous, unbelievably bright and great fun to be with—she's totally unique.

Yet like many nonperforming legends, Aileen is better known for her pen than for her person. As Suzy Knickerbocker, America's top syndicated society columnist, her name is recognized by nearly everyone, but not her face. I always considered that rather a shame, since she cuts as glamorous a figure as any Hollywood star.

I'd known Suzy for years, so when she was approved by the clients at their annual meeting in Milwaukee, I couldn't wait to call her. She was delighted and accepted on the spot.

The day of the shooting, she arrived at Bill King's studio with her fabulous jewels and her equally fabulous smile. It was clear that she need not have depended entirely on her brains and wit to get ahead. She's a natural in front of the camera. We decided to try a sexy shot—"but then you knew that," as Suzy always says in her column.

What becomes a Legend most?

Blackglama

Claudette Colbert had met Liv Ullmann at Helen and Bob Bernstein's and pronounced her charming. I'd always wanted her for the campaign, and now that she was in New York, appearing on Broadway in *Anna Christie,* the timing was perfect. Plus, I had a contact—and ally—in Claudette.

I called John Springer, the agent who represents many of these legendary ladies, to ask if she'd be interested. Her initial reaction was noncommittal.

Claudette and I decided to see the play, and after the performance we went backstage to talk to the star. She was—and is—unbelievable, with the most seductive eyes I've ever seen. She has an amazing ability to focus on you as though you were the only person in the room—or in the world.

Claudette introduced me and explained that I represented Blackglama, adding that she herself had posed for the campaign and hoped Liv would too. Miss Ullmann agreed to do it then and there, and I left the theater completely smitten.

The photo session took place at Bill King's studio. Ullmann wore her good-luck necklace—a thin gold chain with a small diamond in the center—and our mink.

Liv Ullmann is famous for her close-ups, and with a face like hers, it's easy to understand why. So Bill turned on the fan and came in close, snapping her with her long hair blowing, her remarkable eyes caressing the camera.

Later, I took proofs of the shot backstage after a performance to show her. She took one look and exclaimed, "You've made me so beautiful, no one will recognize me!"

It's a haunting photograph and drew tremendous response from the public. To this day, I can't see those eyes without vividly remembering the lady, and wondering how the camera could have captured her so perfectly. I can only suppose that Bill responded to her the same way I did.

What becomes a Legend most?

Blackglama

Bill Blass asked Diana Vreeland to do the Blackglama campaign for me, and she agreed. The problem was—how to direct a director? Miss Vreeland has directed, and still is engineering, some of the best ideas ever done in fashion. I knew just what I wanted her to do. But would she do it?

She arrived at Bill King's studio with her own Blackglama cape and an assistant carrying her makeup case. Kenneth had already done her hair that afternoon, but she proceeded to make herself up at the studio. Miss Vreeland is famous for rubbing rouge on her face in exactly the right places, and we all stood watching in awe as she applied it. At one point, she looked in the mirror and examined her hair. "Isn't one side sticking out farther than the other?" she asked. We all agreed that it was. Without pausing for a moment, she said, "Well that's the way it's supposed to be." If perfect is never perfect, who would know better than Vreeland?

I sketched what I had visualized for the ad. I knew it had to be the most dramatic picture of all time because that's who she is—every Vreeland gesture is drama.

When I showed her the sketch, she said, "It's not me; I wouldn't do that. But you're the director—go ahead and direct me."

So she stood and held her hand up while I held the cape (in some of the contacts you can see *my* hand), and we cropped the picture to catch just the right pose. She looks as if she ruled the world.

Several days later, I took the photograph to her office in the Metropolitan Museum. I sat before her desk thinking, She may hate it, but the picture is absolutely right. She opened her desk drawer, pulled out a magnifying glass and studied it for a while. Then she looked up at me and said, "Young man, you know what you are doing."

She has since said that Michelangelo must have done the retouching; but even if Michelangelo were alive, he could not improve on Diana Vreeland. She needs no help from anyone.

What becomes a Legend most?

Blackglama

Monday morning and all was not well. *Vogue, Bazaar* and *Town & Country* were already demanding plates of the Faye Dunaway ad. If they didn't get them by Friday night, we'd wind up running blank pages, to the tune of about a hundred thousand dollars.

"Call the magazines and ask for an extension," I instructed my production man, Rocky Piliero. "If we get her today, we'll make it."

We'd had difficulty in contacting Miss Dunaway to pose for the campaign, and we were way behind schedule. Even so, I was determined to get her. She's the closest thing we've got to those wonderful, glamorous stars of the forties and fifties—Crawford, Dietrich, Davis, Colbert. A legend with staying power. Her performance in *Chinatown* sold me on her, though we didn't actually ask her to pose until she'd won the Oscar for *Network.*

I nervously tried to construct the week ahead. If we photographed Dunaway today, we'd be in good shape for fall insertions. "Just please, please let Dunaway show," I beseeched the gods of Madison Avenue, who oversee these things.

I arrived at the studio late and to my great relief was told that Miss Dunaway was already in the dressing room. I went in to meet her. She sat quietly, hair tied back, being made-up, wearing only jeans and a blue and white striped T-shirt.

I waited an hour, then Dunaway appeared looking like, well, like Dunaway. In a word, breath-taking. On the set she was the professional, the legend, in fact more so. It was one of the most interesting sessions we've ever had—it lasted for almost two hours. Both Bill and Miss Dunaway were determined to get a legendary photograph.

When the contact sheets arrived (Bill rushed them over the moment they were ready), I knew the results were worth everything. The photographs were spectacular. We chose a really glamorous shot with lots of skin, but Dunaway hated it. "Too sexy," she said and she proved to be right. She ultimately selected the shot herself, one which she felt captured the essence of the whole campaign and most truly expressed herself. So if it is the best ad of the whole campaign—and many people think it is—we owe it all to Faye Dunaway.

What becomes a Legend most?

Blackglama

Claudette Colbert was Blackglama's first double legend. Bill King took the photograph just days after her seventy-fifth birthday, in what must have been the shortest photo session in history. The lady hates having her picture taken!

At the time, Colbert was returning to Broadway, after a sixteen-year absence, in *The Kingfisher,* with Rex Harrison and George Rose. I knew the play would be a smash and that a new ad now would be good publicity for the show and for my client too.

Claudette loved the photograph—one of the few times I've heard her say that. And so did the mink breeders who make up the Blackglama association, despite the fact that they've complained from time to time about the lack of youth in the campaign.

I invited a group of twenty-five visiting mink breeders and their wives to see their legend in action on the stage. Afterward, I took them backstage to meet Claudette in person. As we were leaving, one of them turned to me and said, "Well, you did it."

"Did what?" I asked, puzzled.

"You finally got a young person to do the campaign."

What becomes a Legend most?

Blackglama

If ever Hollywood had a perfect lady, it was Joan Fontaine. Refined, well bred—was there ever anyone like her?

I collected her at her Manhattan apartment by limo, of course, and was delighted to find her as pretty in person as on the screen. We drove directly to Bill King's—and once we arrived, confusion reigned. Where is the hairdresser? What hairdresser? Quick, somebody get a hairdresser! Nothing like that had ever happened before. Miss Fontaine remained calm, but I was a wreck. I called the Vidal Sassoon Salon (a client) and pleaded to have someone sent instantly. By the time the stylist arrived, however, Miss Fontaine was already on the set. She'd done her hair herself. She has the professionalism of all those great legends of the screen. And when we fell down on the job, she came through like the trouper she is.

Miss Fontaine later told me that she'd been especially pleased to pose for the campaign because to her it represented a last stronghold of glamour and the soigné way of life that used to be. "It seems there's just no room left for elegance in this paper-plate, blue-jean world," she complained. "And I, for one, think it's a shame."

We chose a classic Fontaine pose for the ad, deliberately different from the shot used on her already published autobiography, except for the Blackglama she wore. Seeing that photo, I couldn't help wondering if she'd been trying to tell us something.

When the ad ran, her friends reacted with what she jokingly termed "polite jealousy." "The photograph is wonderful" she told me. "I look like a thirty-year-old chorus girl. And while I may be one," she laughed, "I'm not the other."

What becomes a Legend most?

Blackglama

I called Helen Hayes direct—simply rang her home—and to my surprise she answered the phone herself. I recognized her voice instantly and I stammered through an introduction while I struggled to regain my composure. After all, I kept thinking, this *is* the first lady of the American theater. I finally blurted out my request. "I thought you'd never call!" she exclaimed. "You've done all my friends—Mary and Ethel—and I wondered if you'd ever get to me!"

"When are you free?" I asked.

"Let's do it now before you change your mind," she joked.

Later that week, I sent a car and an escort to her Rockland County, New York, home. I didn't meet her myself until she arrived at Bill King's. She's a tiny, white-haired Irish lady with an amazing twinkle in her eye and a great sense of humor.

The makeup man could barely get her done between his questions about every star in Hollywood. He was the type that knew the color of Rita Hayworth's nail polish in every movie she ever made. Miss Hayes went along, but I could see her growing slightly impatient with this interrogation. Finally he gushed, "Miss Hayes, you look so wonderful. How do you do it? Is it health food?"

"Health food, hmph!" she replied. "It's John Travolta, *Saturday Night Fever* and Big Macs." That formula may not work for everyone, but it has certainly worked for Helen Hayes.

What becomes a Legend most?

Blackglama

Renata Scotto is not only a brilliant opera star, but an unparalleled actress. So once she'd agreed to appear in the campaign, I knew we'd have no trouble obtaining a marvelous photograph.

What I was unprepared for was the way she looked when she arrived at the studio. She's always been a small woman, stout in the manner of many great divas. But here she was looking positively svelte. She said she'd gone on a diet after seeing her television performance in *La Bohème*. "I hadn't realized how fat I'd become," she told me. "Mamma mia! I looked terrible—even next to Pavarotti!" She'd lost forty pounds and proved you don't need bulk to hit the high notes.

I'd asked her to bring her own jewelry for the picture and she produced masses of it, the most beautiful Italianate pieces you've ever seen. On the set, Bill King turned his usual fan on her, to an unusual reaction. "Mamma mia," she complained, "you'll ruin my voice with that fan in my face."

Scotto began miming along to one of her recordings, but Bill, always the perfectionist, wasn't satisfied. He wanted her to sing—really sing—to get a realistic performing shot. Miss Scotto was trying to save her voice, but briefly complied. In her best operatic style, she burst into a few stirring phrases from *Don Giovanni,* complete with her own improvised lyrics. "Mozzarella, pizza pie," she sang. "I'm-a so hungry I could-a die!" The place broke up, but Bill got his shot.

She loved the picture and so did I, though we had a tough time selecting a pose we could be certain her fans would recognize. Interestingly, when she went to Christie Brothers to select her coat, she tried on every one they had and finally settled on the cape she'd worn in the photograph. It was one of the few times we'd chosen exactly right.

What becomes a Legend most?

Blackglama

Angela Lansbury once sang in *The Picture of Dorian Gray.* I saw that movie when I was eleven years old and didn't sleep for a week. And I never forgot Angela Lansbury. She's a star who became a legend rather late in her career. Most people think of *Mame* —but for me it was her brilliant performance in *Something for Everyone,* a hilarious film almost no one but me has ever seen.

I went to see her in a Sunday-afternoon preview of *Sweeney Todd,* which would become the season's hot Broadway ticket. During the first intermission, I asked Ruth Mitchell, Hal Prince's associate director, if Miss Lansbury would be interested in posing for the campaign. She asked, and Lansbury agreed. I was delighted. However, we almost never got to photograph her. During the second act, a heavy piece of scenery crashed to the stage just inches from where she stood. Lansbury never missed a beat, though the show had to be temporarily stopped to move the debris.

The day of the shoot, Lansbury arrived fully made up with her own hairdresser in tow. We had a preconceived notion of how we wanted her—as "Mame" as possible, with tons of Bulgari jewels and mountains of Blackglama.

We never did find the coat we were looking for, so we improvised, pinning hundreds of mink tails to a Blackglama shrug. The effect was wonderful, though we eventually toned down the jewelry. Miss Lansbury was a marvelous subject. She's known for her wit, and she didn't disappoint.

I brought a proof of the photograph backstage after a performance for her approval, and she adored it. We toasted it with champagne. At this writing, the public's reaction is still to be determined. But with a legend like Lansbury, how can we miss?

What becomes a Legend most?

Blackglama

BLACKGLAMA® IS THE WORLD'S FINEST NATURAL DARK RANCH MINK BRED ONLY IN AMERICA BY THE GREAT LAKES MINK MEN